Everything I Know
I Learned from Baseball

About the Author

Philip Theibert has been around baseball his entire life, starting as a batboy for Chapman College. He was a catcher in college and has the crooked fingers to prove it. Philip also coached summer league baseball for years, making him a third-generation baseball coach.

Philip has an extensive writing background and views himself much like an utility infielder, with the ability to write at many positions. He has worked as a speechwriter, copywriter, reporter, editor, technical writer, and poet.

Philip's books include two collections of baseball poems: *Collisions at Home* and *Bunts*. His articles have appeared in the *Wall Street Journal*, *Writer's Digest, Toast Masters, Vital Speeches, Manager's Journal*, and other publications. He is a Pushcart Prize nominee.

Philip currently lives in Birmingham, Alabama, and spends summer evenings rooting for the Birmingham Barons. His daughter teaches in New Orleans, and his son has the misfortune of being a Twins fan.

Everything I Know
I Learned from Baseball

99 Life Lessons from the Ball Field

by Philip Theibert

SUMMER
GAME
BOOKS

ISBN: 978-1-938545-66-5 (hc)
ISBN: 978-1-938545-67-2 (ebook)
ISBN: 978-1-938545-34-4 (pbk)

For permission requests, and for information regarding bulk purchases or additional distribution, write to the publisher at

info@summergamebooks.com or

Summer Game Books
Attn: Walter Friedman
PO Box 818
South Orange, NJ 07079

To Dick Theibert and the boys of Chapman College.

Acknowledgments

A special thanks to Walt Friedman of Summer Game Books, whose insights and expertise made this a much better book.

Contents

9 Independence 127

Quotation Sources 143

1

Attitude

Baseball is 50% from the neck up.
—Ted Williams

Think Positive, Be Positive

Managers and fans like players with good attitudes. Sportswriter John Kieran once pointed out that although Lou Gehrig set numerous records, "his greatest record was his absolute reliability. He could be counted on—ALWAYS. He was there every day at the ballpark bending his back and ready to break his neck to help his side win. Day after day, year after year. He never sulked or whined or put himself before his team. He was the answer to a manager's dream."

Another Yankees all-time great, Casey Stengel, knew something about dedication and a positive attitude, which made hard-nosed Hank Bauer one of his favorite players. Stengel said, "That fella [Hank] Bauer, he had qualities of which there were four. He'd report on time. He was there for practice, and he would fight the whole season—with all that was in his body."

In life, first and foremost, you have to be there, and to succeed, you have to be prepared. Show up early and take extra ground balls or work on your bunting. Care about your appearance and the effort you put forth. Keep your shirt tucked in and run to your position. Always hustle, always do your best.

A positive attitude, combined with hustle, is a powerful recipe for achieving success, whether it's on the job, with a project, or building relationships.

Be Confident

Be eager to step into the batter's box so you can show your stuff. Go up to bat thinking you will get a hit. If you strikeout or pop up, chalk it up to experience and be proud for giving it your best. Confidence will help you in every endeavor in life. When you think you're going to strike out in baseball or in life, you'll probably prove yourself right. When you doubt yourself, you dig a hole that is tough to climb out of.

If you want the ball to be hit to you because you know you'll make the play, you're probably right about that, too. Believing in yourself is the foundation for others to believe in you, too. If you don't, how can you expect others to do so?

Bounce Back

Baseball is challenging. There are many ways to succeed, but there are also many ways to fail. You will strike out; you will make an error; you will get thrown out stealing. It's how you deal with those failures and what you learn from them that matters.

Dave Winfield said, "You have to understand that life and baseball are littered with all kinds of obstacles and problems along the way. You have to learn how to overcome them to be successful in life."

Because baseball is as much a game of failure as it is of success, you must turn the setbacks into teaching moments. Learn the lessons they hold and move on. Watch the ball into your glove, lay off high pitches, always check the coach for signs, and make yourself a better player by building on your failures as well as your successes.

Every Day Is a New Opportunity

Bob Feller once said, "Every day is a new opportunity. You can build on yesterday's success or put its failures behind and start over again." That's part of the beauty of baseball. It's a long season. You can put a bad game behind you because there will be another game tomorrow. You can put a bad at-bat behind you because soon it will be your turn again.

Life is like that, too. The sun will rise tomorrow and with it will come new opportunities. Don't look back at yesterday's failure, wishing you had done this or that instead. Look ahead to today's game, today's challenge, and get ready to do your best.

We All Are Listed Day to Day

When a player is injured, we often hear that he is listed "day to day." But when you think about it, aren't we all? No one knows what tomorrow will bring, so you'd better make the most out of today. If you accept that, in a way, we are all listed day to day, that our health and happiness can vanish in a moment, how would you live your life differently? Maybe you wouldn't put off that difficult task until tomorrow; maybe you wouldn't wait until it's too late to tell someone how much you care.

I learned this lesson the hard and painful way while driving young ballplayers back from a game. I don't remember a drunk barreling through a red light, his van crushing the small Honda we were driving. I don't remember the hospital, or even the trip home after. The ballplayers and I recovered, but what never left me was the feeling that we are all listed day to day.

Life, like baseball, provides opportunities for happiness and success. But it doesn't go on forever. A game lasts only nine innings. Seize opportunities when they arise; don't hesitate. Don't put off trying to steal. Who knows when you will get on base again?

It's Only a Game

People blow things out of proportion. The smallest things can take on enormous importance in our hearts and minds. A great example is parents in the stands watching their child's game. Countless kids have cringed watching their mom and dad make fools of themselves over a bad call or other small problem.

Bert Blyleven recalled being upset after giving up his first major league home run at age 19. His manager, Bill Rigney, consoled him with some simple, sage advice: "Take it easy. That's not the last home run you're going to give up." Blyleven went on to allow more than 400 in his Hall of Fame career.

Keep things in perspective. If you lose, or your kid gets a raw deal, don't let it make you crazy. The sun will come up tomorrow. There will be another game. There will be situations in your life when bosses, co-workers, in-laws, spouses, or your teenagers will lose their sense of perspective, and will make themselves and you miserable over something that is just not important. Keep yours. When

means you are stuck in the whirlpool of your own emotions, and you'd rather keep spinning in them than admit you are wrong. You can only grow as a person when you let go of responsibility, when you stop—as they say in baseball—blaming the ump.

Keep It Fun

A somewhat depressing statistic is that 70% of ballplayers stop playing by the age of 13. Perhaps it is parental pressure to succeed, perhaps the coach is a dictator, perhaps it is simply that baseball is not fun for them; it is more like a job. I suspect that many kids leave baseball for activities that are more "fun."

As a coach, I held my kids to a high standard of excellence. They worked hard, but I always made sure we had one fun activity at the end of every practice. For example, we would have a hitting contest, with me pitching, and the team batting. If, as a team, they got more than two hits, I had to run around the field. If they got two hits or less, they had to run around the field. Sometimes I won, sometimes they won.

I learned long ago that if you are the boss, you can't keep driving your employees. You have to stop and have fun every now and then. A simple activity can increase morale and build teamwork far better than a long, boring meeting.

The baseball season, like life, is short. Relish your time on the field. Enjoy the sun, spitting sunflower seeds, chewing gum, bending your hat brim, playing catch, the smell of glove oil, sliding into second, rounding third at full speed, cheering on your teammates. Be a part of the moment. Appreciate the details.

Think about the best moments of your life. Chances are, 90 percent of them were not earth-shaking events. Our fondest recollections often involve small pleasures: coffee with a friend, a walk on the first nice day of spring, being greeted at the door by your dog, tail wagging, watching your child ride his or her first bike, or maybe hearing your favorite song at just the right time.

In life, like baseball, there are very few game-saving catches and walk-off home runs. Take satisfaction from doing the basics the right way every day, from hitting the cutoff man, to being in the right place to make a play. If we spend our time dreaming about being the big hero, we miss all the small moments that add up to true satisfaction.

Develop a Sense of Purpose

The question becomes, as a coach—how do you get baseball players, or as a business person—your staff, or as a parent—your children, to *want* to give 100 percent, so that full effort is heartfelt and comes from within, not because you are yelling at them or offering a reward?

How does "going all out" become ingrained in your value system? Whether it's on the field, in business, or at home, we must instill a sense of purpose in the tasks at hand and the goals that need to be achieved.

Giving someone a sense of purpose ties what they are doing to something larger, to something besides themselves. If there is no sense of obligation to your team or community or partner, life becomes every man for himself.

A classic example a buffalo herd. At one time, no one was "in charge" of buffalo herds, and every man shot as many buffalo as he could. After all, the more buffalo men shot, the more money they made selling hides. There was no sense of obligation to preserve the buffalo, no vision beyond immediate gratification, no greater purpose; the only objective was to make money. Before long, there were not enough buffalo around for anyone to make a living.

You always want to break down selfish thinking in any community endeavor. To instill a sense of team-work and shared purpose in any team or group, you must elevate their contributions beyond the daily routine imbue it with a sense of purpose. The result will be happier colleagues and happier teammates, which will lead to greater productivity, and more victories on the field.

Celebrate Small Victories

I love baseball because it provides us with many small victories along the way. Laying off a bad pitch, backing up an errant throw, hitting the ball hard—even if it turns into an out. There are so many small things that don't show up on the scorecard but show you are in the game all the way.

It is very rare for someone to hit a home run or strike out the side, so smart ballplayers and focused teams know how to celebrate the small pitch-to-pitch, inning-to-inning, and day-to-day victories.

Focus on the small triumphs and the big victories will come. Take pride in accomplishing them, and celebrate small victories with your teammates to grow team spirit and to boost morale.

What small victories can you celebrate with your family or with your team, whatever team that might be? Give yourself credit for doing what needs to be done, and praise your teammates or colleagues for their everyday accomplishments, too. What thing that might be taken for granted can you acknowledge that will make someone feel better today?

2

Preparation

The key step for an infielder is the first
one, but before the ball is hit.
—Earl Weaver

Master the Basics

Dick Williams put it succinctly: "Fundamentals are the most valuable tools a player can possess. Bunt the ball into the ground. Hit the cutoff man. Take the extra base. Learn the fundamentals."

Every job and activity in life requires basic skills. Master them and you will have built a foundation for excellence. People will trust you because it will be clear you know what you are doing and that you have put in the time and effort to learn how to do things right. Relying on instinct or smarts to do a job or conduct business may make you look brilliant once in a while, but you'll probably hit a wall when you reach that unexpected curve in the road.

It's like relying on talent alone to play a sport. A great arm or speed can make up for a lack of technical knowledge, but at some point you'll be playing against equally talented people and your lack of skills will show.

Fundamentals are the foundation of all success. Without them, exceptional performance and accomplishments cannot be achieved, nor can long-term success.

Anticipate

Don't wait for something to happen and then react; try to figure it out before it happens. Where will a lefty batter hit the ball off a left-handed fireballer? What is that speedy base runner going to do? Use situations to anticipate where the ball is going and what your opponent is going to do.

In life, if you know where the ball is going, you'll be the one to catch it. If you get outside your thoughts and worries, you will be ahead of the crowd, not part of it.

The great Henry Aaron said, "Guessing what the pitcher is going to throw is 80% of being a successful hitter. The other 20% is just execution."

Know Where to Throw the Ball

There is an old saying in baseball: Anyone can catch a fly ball. Knowing where to throw it when you do makes you a ballplayer.

Let's say there are runners on first and third, one out, and a fly ball comes to you. Do you go home to cut off the run, or to second to keep the runner out of scoring position? To know the answer before the ball arrives, you have to consider all the variables: How fast are the runners? What is the score and inning? How strong is your arm?

Situations like this occur in every game for every player on the field. If you wait for a situation to happen and then figure out what to do, many times you will act too late, and your decision will be the wrong one.

In life, everyone gets opportunities. Sometimes the ball is going to get hit to you. The question is, how do you make the most of that opportunity? Where do you throw that fly ball after you catch it?

Something Always Happens

Mike Schmidt once said, "Any time you think you have the game conquered, the game will turn around and punch you right in the nose."

When I coached summer league baseball, we had a standing joke. When we had a lead, one coach would look at the other and say, "OK, what's going to happen?" And usually something did. The other team would hit a home run; we would make three errors, throw to the wrong base, get picked off. Things happened.

Never expect the status quo to remain. Always ask yourself "What could happen?" By asking the question, you take the first step to prepare yourself for the unexpected.

Let's say you have what seems to be a secure job. What could happen? The company could have a bad year, a recession could hit, layoffs could come. By anticipating what could happen, you put yourself in a position to prepare for possible layoffs by polishing up the resume, getting additional training, maybe saving more of your paycheck. In short, you prepare for what *could* happen.

Have a Game Plan

If you are facing a pitcher who throws heat, don't swing at anything above the waist. Chances are you won't catch up with it. Make him get the ball down. If his control is iffy, make him throw strikes and tire him out by working the count. If your opponent has a lot of speed, you should play the infield in, hold the runners close, work on pickoff plays.

What is your game plan when you are going to a tryout, preparing for an exam, heading to a job interview? Invest ample time beforehand to run through the issues and challenges of the upcoming challenge. Apply your experience to what you are likely to be confronted with. Think of the strengths you bring to the situation. Don't go in there cold; have a plan, your own plan, and stick with it.

Plant a Seed

My father was a great believer that you could "remote control" umpires, and that any coach that did not "remote control" the umpires was not doing his job.

To "plant a seed" with the umpire, every now and then my father would challenge their calls. He wouldn't start an argument or show disrespect. He would simply state his point and leave.

My father believed that if he made his case reasonably the umpire wasn't going to change the call that time, but the next close play may end up going in his favor.

The same approach can work with your manager at a job, your coach, and even your mate. Perhaps you have an idea that's going to take some convincing to make happen. Try planting a seed, maybe with a short conversation in the elevator or at the breakfast table. Try to shape the mindset of the other person to make him or her more receptive to your idea.

If the idea has merit, those first points should stick with the other person. The next time you bring it up they'll have had some time to become familiar with your idea, and maybe even mulled it over a bit. By the time you go for the sell, it may have become their idea!

Know the Rules

If you go out and argue with the umpire that your hitter should not have been out because the shortstop dropped the ball, and the umpire looks at you in disbelief and says, "Infield fly rule," you will look like an idiot, and more importantly, you will lose the umpire's respect.

They say there is no such thing as a stupid question, but "they" may be the stupid ones for being so simplistic. If you keep asking dumb questions of your teacher when the answer can be found in the instructions for the assignment, how does that make you look? Stupid or lazy, or both?

The rules of play, just like the rules of the road or school, are even more fundamental than the fundamentals. You need to know them to avoid costly mistakes, and to earn the respect of your peers. This is particularly important if you are in a position of leadership.

Don't Get Surprised by What You Should Know

When playing at a strange ballpark, a smart outfielder does not just trot out to his position and start playing. He does his research, prepares for what might happen, and makes sure he will not be surprised by what he should know. A good outfielder will determine how the ball comes off the wall, how it comes out of the corner. He will make note of how long the grass is, if it's wet. He will look for changes in sun and wind.

During the game, the prepared outfielder will always know when the tying or winning run is at bat or on base. He will know who has great speed and who doesn't. He will have studied the hitters in practice and their stances, so he knows who pulls and who hits with power. He will then play accordingly.

In short, a good outfielder is determined not to be surprised by "what he should know." And by "should know," I mean what he can know by doing his homework and paying attention. The same can be done by every player at every position.

Think of your own life—the work you do, the people you know, the challenging or competitive situations you will be involved in during your pursuit of success and happiness. Assemble your knowledge and experience and think through possible scenarios and how you can best deal with them. If you get surprised when something does happen, whose fault is that?

First Impressions Matter

The umpire runs the game. He sets the tone, and you expect him to look professional. What if he doesn't run to cover a play at a base? What if his shoes are not shined, his shirt is not tucked in, and he is always taking water breaks, even during an inning? What message is he sending to the crowd, the managers, the players?

What kind of first impressions are you making, in your classes, for instance? Let's say you are working on your first paper that involves research. Simply put, the quality and content of the work will establish in the teacher's mind that quality of work that you can do. If key points are not properly supported, if the paper is full of grammatical and spelling errors, what does this say about the quality of work you are likely to do in the future? If you don't put your best foot forward at the outset, you are creating an expectation of failure or mediocrity that will be difficult to overcome.

Visualize

An important skill for all pitchers is visualizing, seeing themselves throwing the pitch before they actually throw it. This skill can be acquired by practice. It works something like this: Ask the pitcher about pitch selection, location, and target for the pitch he wants to throw.

The pitcher should then describe in detail where he will locate the pitch, at what speed, and at what angle. This will make him establish in his mind where he wants the ball to go and how. Then the pitcher needs to close his eyes briefly and visualize the pitch in his mind happening exactly the way he wants it to.

Training your mind to picture success helps train your muscles to execute that success. When you visualize what you want to happen—not just think about it—you eliminate mental distractions and help rein in errant thoughts that cause you to drift away from your goal.

Visualizing success can be done in many aspects of life. In fact, the ability to focus is probably even more important outside the realm of baseball and sports than within it, because there are many more distractions in the real world. If you do not visualize what you want out of an interview or training regimen, and zero in on your objectives, goals can become fuzzy and doubts can take over.

Know Your Tools

A baseball player is judged on the classic five tools of baseball. They are speed, arm strength, fielding, hitting, and hitting for power. These are the classic yardsticks of ability, whether you are in Little League or a Major League prospect.

The five-tool rule applies to many areas of life, for example, preparing for a big test: You could say the five tools include understanding what type of exam it will be, reviewing relevant class notes, doing required reading, getting adequate rest the night before, and arriving early so you don't have to rush. Breaking down goals and skills you want to develop into five parts is a great way to frame a plan of action and set priorities for yourself.

Look at other challenges in your life and think "What five tools do I need to be successful?" Write out some ideas and play with them until you come up with five pillars. Then assess where you are in terms of accomplishing them.

3

Focus

Focus on your goals, not your fears.
—Roy Bennett, writer

Collect Yourself

A pick-off attempt is made. You dive back into first. Call time, brush yourself off, straighten your hat. Then take your lead again. You find yourself behind in the count 0-2. Step out. Take a breath. Don't get on the defensive and let the pitcher dictate the pace.

Whatever the situation—before a tryout or a challenging test or a difficult confrontation—learn to take small moments to collect yourself, to clear your head and lock in your focus, so you can do your best and give yourself the best chance to succeed.

Stay Calm

My father, a college baseball coach for years, said there were three basic rules of pitching. "Work fast, throw strikes, keep your cool." What good does it do to get upset? All your focus and energy gets channeled to your anger instead of finding solutions. And when you are upset, you upset those around you.

Is that what a parent, coach, a leader—or anyone in a position of responsibility—should do? React to a challenge by getting upset? If you are a pitcher and you're angry about walking the last batter, you are not concentrating on the next batter, who can hurt you more than the man on base. This same thing happens in golf every day on every golf course. One bad shot can ruin a golfer's whole round. He loses his cool, loses his concentration, and next loses the ball in the water! Think three simple words and etch them in your brain: GET OVER IT! No matter what happens, stay calm and focus on the task at hand.

You Can Observe a Lot by Watching

Baseball is complicated. So are people. It's just like Yogi said: "You can observe a lot by watching." And you can learn a lot, too. Don't goof off on the bench. Use that time to see what the pitcher is throwing, where the fielders are positioned, who has a good arm and who doesn't. See if you can pick up tendencies in opposing batters or pitchers. Watch the base runners. Did they miss a base or tag up too soon? You can make down time wasted time, or you can use it to learn something, to grow. Choose learning.

Diffuse Pressure

A good ballplayer realizes that pressure comes from within. Can't throw strikes? As Satchel Paige said, "Home plate don't move." In other words, it is not the situation that makes you tense, that makes the plate move around, it's you.

What is the difference between an ordinary game and the final game of a tournament? The ball is the same, the bases are the same distant apart, a fly ball is still just a fly ball. In *Hoosiers*, when Gene Hackman's team makes the state tournament, he has his players measure the height of the basket. Everything is exactly the same as their home gym, of course.

How do you learn to handle pressure? Turn it back into an ordinary situation. Put things in perspective. Let your mind relax. Be consistent in your thoughts, actions, and reactions. Shrink down whatever the challenge is to its actual size, make it just another game or at-bat; make that interview just another conversation. If you have developed good habits and practiced your skills, you can trust your abilities, and they will carry you through any situation.

Study Situations for a Solution

There is always a way out of a jam and a best way to deal with a problem. Should you intentionally walk someone, throw a changeup to induce a double play, move in to help make the play at home, guard the line to take away the extra base hit?

Every problem has a solution. There is a best way to overcome every challenge, a "best practice" for every situation. Take a moment and use your knowledge and experience to find that best way. Don't just set out on a path blindly because you feel you need to do something right away. Whether it's baseball or life, investing time and thought before taking action will save you time and energy, and lead you to greater success than those who do not keep their cool.

Be Alert

There will be long innings, deliberate pitchers, lots of bases on balls. Keep your head in the game! That's why catchers yell how many outs there are, why there's infield chatter, why you throw the ball around the horn after an out. Watch how the catcher shifts behind the plate to help anticipate where the ball is going. Watch the batter's swing or where he's looking. Constantly remind yourself of the game situation and think about what you will do if the ball comes to you.

Baseball trains you to be constantly vigilant, forces you to maintain your focus so you are ready no matter what happens next, whenever that next may be. Try to be the same way in life. Don't lapse into daydreams and fantasies; don't let routine deaden your awareness. You never know when life will hit you a hot two-hopper or throw you a proverbial curve.

Pay Attention to Details

If you are on first base, check the pitcher's heel. A right-handed pitcher has to lift his back heel before he throws over. If you know that, there is no reason you should ever be picked off by a righty.

Is the wind blowing out or blowing in? Is the grass fast or slow? What kind of cloud cover can you expect during the game?

Think about your own life—your family, your schoolwork, your job. Give them a fresh look and see what you notice. Is there something you could be doing a little differently? Are there signs you are missing from your teacher, your coach, or maybe your boyfriend or girlfriend? Sometimes big messages can be sent in small, subtle ways, and it's the people who notice those little things who get the best jump on situations and who head off problems while they are still small.

Learn from the Lineup Card

The lineup card tells what position each player is playing, and more importantly, in what order they are hitting. A lot of thought goes into developing the batting order, putting getting on base skill and speed at the top, power in the middle, maybe some balancing of lefty/righty batters. The lineup is a way to maximize a team's strengths, minimize its weaknesses, and find combinations to get the most out of the group. The lineup brings order, strategy, and structure to a team, and provides a framework/road map for how you're going to play the game.

When your life is in chaos, when you are struggling, do you have a lineup card for yourself? Can you assess your strengths and weakness, identify your opponent or obstacles, and make a lineup of action to establish structure and discipline, to give yourself the best chance possible to succeed?

See the Bigger Picture

Coaches and many parents get so caught up in baseball that they forget it is just a game and the final score will not be featured on ESPN. Plus, parents tend to forget that the odds of a high school player even making a college team are less than six percent. Even worse, the odds of a high school ballplayer making the big leagues is one in 6,600, or 0.015 percent. That's roughly the chance of a thief guessing your PIN number on the first try.

So why do some coaches encourage kids to "play through pain?" The word stupid comes to mind. Last time I checked, pain is a warning sign of injury and ignoring pain frequently leads to greater injury. Also, many parents brag that their kid plays on the school team, the summer league team, and the travel team, etc. Children who play on more than one team are at risk for injuries caused by repetitive stress put on the same part of the body. Injuries that look like sprains in adults can be fractures in children. Children are more susceptible to fractures because their bones are still growing.

The recent escalation of travel ball, elite teams, and tougher competition comes with a price of pain. A simple philosophy when it comes to children and baseball is "No pain, no pain." Coaches must make sure to keep the experience of playing ball fun!

Know your limits and the limits of your players. The same philosophy applies to work or in any relationship, especially how you interact with your family. Push too hard and the fun disappears, motivation is lost, resentment can take over. Instead of inspiring someone to greater heights, you drag them down, maybe even set them back further than they would have been with no outside motivation at all.

Recognize the Spin

A curveball has a different spin than a fastball. It comes out of the pitcher's hand differently than a fastball. The pitcher may have a different release point for each pitch, a different arm motion, and if you watch carefully enough, you may even notice that he holds the ball differently in his hand depending on which pitch he is going to throw.

Try to figure out what the pitcher is throwing you. Zero in on the finest details and see all you can see. Don't let the pitcher dictate the action. Give yourself whatever edge you can get.

People will challenge and throw ideas at you your whole life. Watch their delivery; pick up on the clues they provide to figure out where they are coming from and what they might do next. Watch the "spin" they put on their words and how they approach you. Doing so will make it much easier to assess their motives and goals to meet the challenges they present or to connect with them to build a better relationship.

Go to the Right Source

Many coaches charge out to the field to start an argument with the wrong umpire. Go to the umpire who made the call! He is the one who can do something about it. No umpire wants to overrule another, and will rarely do so. So if you are hoping to get your way using that approach you will be out of luck and just look like a fool.

The same thing happens in daily life. You're an unhappy customer berating a customer service person who just responds by the book and has no decision-making power. You announce that you want to see their supervisor. Doing so, however, puts the supervisor in a bad position because she wants to support her employee.

When you do this, you make the customer service person like the umpire who will not overrule another umpire. You create a situation that is difficult for everyone. But if you had gone directly to the store manager, the person who could actually help, you would be much more likely to get satisfaction and not put the customer service rep and her supervisor in a bad spot.

Don't Miss the Signals

When you are batting, you are supposed to step out of the batter box or at least look over at the third base coach every pitch to see if any plays are on. If you are on base, you are supposed to do the same, in case a hit and run, bunt, or a steal has been called. The batter and baserunners must be on the "same page" as the coach. If a third base coach flashes a signal and either the base runner or the hitter misses it, opportunities are missed, and outs are made that could have been avoided. Catchers need to constantly check with the bench for defensive signals, sometimes even for pitch calls. A team's strategies are communicated from one or two sources, but must be picked up by the entire team at every point of the game.

Life gives us signals all the time, and it is critical that we pick up on them or problems will be more frequent, and when they arrive we will be less prepared; communication will break down. It is important to pick up the signals the people in your life give off—your boss, your coach, your friends, maybe the person standing behind you in line.

A great deal of communication occurs without words, at times intentionally, at times very subtly. Messages are often sent in small gestures or a change of expression, and if we are aware of them, it can help us understand what others are feeling and provide insight on how we may better connect with them.

Be attuned to the signals being sent by the people and situations in your life. How are your relationships and how you do at school and with friends affected when you miss those signals? Missed signals in life, much like in baseball, can lead to mistakes and misjudgments that could have been avoided, and can keep you from seizing opportunities and connecting effectively with important people in your life.

4

Character

Baseball gives you every chance to be great. Then it puts every pressure on you to prove that you haven't got what it takes. It never takes away the chance, and it never eases up on the pressure.

—Joe Garagiola

Actions Have Consequences

If you throw a helmet, you sit out two innings. You use a cuss word, you sit out a whole game. Forgetting how many outs there are and getting thrown out can kill an inning and lose a game.

Baseball is a team sport, but the actions of every player on the field can impact the outcome of a game. It is your responsibility to pay attention and do your best. And when you do not, it is just as important that you accept responsibility and commit to yourself that you won't let it happen again.

There are consequences for what you do and how you act. Understand that and own up to them. Doing so is one of the most important steps to maturity, to building your character.

It's the same thing in life, except the consequences can be a lot more serious.

Take Responsibility

Don't blame your bat, your glove, the sun, your teammates. They did not make the error; they did not strikeout. You did. Step up, take responsibility, and move on. Doing so will earn you far more respect than making a mistake will take it away. Taking responsibility for a failure today will make it less likely that failure will happen again tomorrow.

Too often parents are like helicopters, hovering over their children. The parents do everything for their kids hoping to help the young ballplayer succeed. But helicopter parents do their children no favors. By shielding them and propping them up, they get in the way of their child's development of a sense of responsibility.

To succeed in baseball or in life, young ballplayers need to learn to motivate themselves, to set their own goals, to establish the inner drive they will need to succeed in life. Even if a child stops playing ball after Little League, if he has learned how to take responsibility for his failures and developed a drive for success, those skills will help him succeed in other endeavors for the rest of his life.

Be a Role Model

Remember that as a coach, you are a role model. If you get into the umpire's personal space, if you yell in his face and jump up and down, the crowd might eat it up, but it shows up the ump and makes YOU the object of derision, not him. And if you toss a fit while coaching youth baseball, what lesson are you teaching the players on your team?

As a player, you can be a role model, too. Top players should set an example for everyone else. If the star shortstop is out there taking extra ground balls, his teammates, who need the work more, will say, "Wow, if he's out there practicing as good as he is, I should be out there, too."

Every player and every person owes it to himself and his colleagues and teammates to set a good example. Good behavior and full effort are contagious, just like bad behavior and lack of effort are.

Parents and older brothers and sisters are like coaches, too. People look up to them and rely on them. Children learn behavior more from observation than any other way. Think before you act and react. If you are hurt or slighted or feel the sting of disrespect, remember that little if anything you say or do occurs in a vacuum; handling a difficult situation effectively can provide a lesson someone dear to you will hold the rest of his or her life.

Shine When No One Is Watching

You do not have to be playing in front of a big crowd to shine. In fact, pride in ourselves is what really makes us shine—the satisfaction of improving and doing things right. When Gary Carter was a paper boy, no one stood on the curb and clapped as he rode by. He was never going to be remembered for setting any paperboy records. After all, last time I checked, there is no Paper Boy Hall of Fame.

But Carter knew the importance of shining for yourself. He said, "I was going to be the best paper boy ever. I used my Sting-Ray bike and got the papers there after school.

People know I porched everything. No roofs, no lawns. I stopped the bike and nailed it. And if I ever missed, I would go pick it up and do it right."

The best ballplayers, and yes, the best students and employees, are the ones who take great pride in doing things the right way for its own sake, not just when coaches or bosses are watching or telling them to. They do things the right way because they know they must look at themselves in the mirror every day, and they want to be happy with what they see.

Prove Something

Nolan Ryan once said, "One of the beautiful things about baseball is that every once in a while you come into a situation where you want to, and where you have to, reach down and prove something." You, too, will face those situations in life—where you must reach down and prove something— to your parent, to your teacher, to your coach, to yourself. Don't run from them. They are opportunities to grow and to find out who you really are.

Earn Your Status

I was a batboy for the college team that my father coached. I was eight years old when I started. The first year I did not have a uniform. We would go to games, and the other team's bat boy had a uniform, but not me. I wore jeans and a T-shirt. Every time I told my father I needed a uniform, he said, "I don't just give out uniforms; you have to earn one."

I worked a whole year as a batboy in regular clothes, and then at Christmas that year I opened a special package. It was my uniform. I must have worn it around the house all day, admiring myself in the mirror.

I'm sure that first day in the uniform would have felt great no matter how or when I got it. But there's no question that I felt prouder, and it looked that much better on me, and that pride and satisfaction were deeper and lasted much longer because I had earned it.

Do More Than Is Required

In my early days as batboy, my father told me a batboy does a lot more than just collect bats. I wanted him to explain the job in detail, but that is all he told me: I would learn as we went along. In the first game, I just picked up bats. But then a foul ball was hit, and my father said, "Aren't you going to get that?" Then one day, my father saw a couple of helmets on the dugout floor, and he asked, "What are those doing there?" I picked them up and put them on the helmet rack.

At that point, I realized that I should be looking around to see what needs to be done, not waiting for it to come to me. By the end of the season, I had expanded my duties to chasing balls, picking up helmets, filling the water cooler, making sure that the lead bat was in the on-deck circle, handing the pitcher his jacket between innings, and keeping the pencil sharp for the scorekeeper. These were all small things, but they added up to a large effect, and I went from being not much more than a spectator to a valuable contributor to the team. Realizing that only made me want to do more.

In life there are many small things we can do—at home, at work, in the community—things to help those around us, even things to help ourselves. When we do the bare minimum, we get minimum satisfaction. When we make the extra effort, we earn the respect and appreciation of others. And most important, we can truly respect ourselves.

Define Yourself

Baseball writers and announcers tell it like it is. If a player hustles, they will praise him for his attitude and approach. If a player makes a mental error or takes it easy on a play, they may question his focus and drive. If a manager makes a dumb move, he will be asked to justify his decision.

Now think about this: What if an announcer or journalist looked at your life? How would he or she describe you? Would you be seen as someone who does his best, someone who gets things done? Or would you be considered a careless person, someone who makes a lot of errors? Do you run the bases of your life going all out, or do you give away at-bats? Find ways to create opportunities rather than waiting for them to knock on your door.

How do you want to be described? What do you want your reputation to be? How hard are you willing to work to earn that reputation?

Define Your Values

There is an old saying: "The problem with having principles is that sooner or later you're going to have to live up to them."

It is easier to make decisions if you are clear on what your values are. One year when I was coaching, our star player, because he was "so good," tried just showing up for games. For a whole week he didn't show up for practice, but come game day on Saturday, there he was. He didn't offer any explanation, just took his glove and went to his regular spot at shortstop. He was shocked when I told him to go sit on the bench. He was not playing that day.

We lost the game, and he would have made a difference if he had played. In fact, halfway through the game, after his

57

replacement had struck out twice, his parents were calling for me to put him in, at least as a pinch hitter. I refused. I firmly believed that if I let him play, the wrong message would be sent to the rest of the kids. They would learn that if you are a star, the rules don't apply to you. It is okay to miss practices.

There is so much to be lost if your players perceive you as choosing favorites, not treating everyone the same. Some will cease to be motivated, and the spirit of the team will suffer. Contributions are needed from the whole team in order to be successful.

Know your values and apply them to all aspects of your life. Base your decisions and actions upon those values. Do not worry about short-term consequences or what people think of you. It is the long-term consequences, the morals and values that you are upholding, that are important, and sticking with them will bring strength to not just you but to others in your life as well.

Put Yourself in Position to Score

It's a good start to be on first or second base, but your ambition must be to reach home. And once you reach base, the best way to score is to be on third.

Think of all the ways you can score from third base that won't get you home from second: A balk. A wild pitch. A passed ball. A bunt or a dribbler. An infield error. A bloop hit. A sacrifice fly. A wild throw by the catcher. A pickoff throw in the dirt. A suicide squeeze bunt. A steal of home. And there are plenty more.

Clearly, if you are on third base, you are in a much better position to reach your goal than if you are on second or first. Getting on base is not enough. You have to maximize your chances to reach your goal, and put yourself in the best position possible to achieve success.

Where are you along the road to success in work, relationships, or even a personal goal—and what are you doing to move yourself down that road? Are you pushing yourself or just coasting? Are you taking a big lead, looking for a short passed ball, thinking about ways you can advance yourself? Or are you just waiting for someone to knock you in? What are the things you need to do to get yourself on third base, where success will be within reach?

Protect Your Players

Sometimes players get angry and argue with an umpire. Hard to believe, isn't it? But as a coach, the last thing you want is for one of your players to be tossed out of a game. So it is the coach's job to go out and separate the player from the umpires and take over the argument. This way, you can defuse the situation and protect your player at the same time. The player won't get tossed out, and you will have shown your players you will stick up for them.

A player's job is to play, and a coach's job is to run his team and represent it in all official capacities. One of those capacities is to support and defend your players during disputes. When they see you are on their side, they will return your loyalty with added effort, thereby strengthening the bonds of the team.

This type of loyalty applies to our family lives as well. Maybe your child is having some trouble in a particular class. Don't be the kind of parent who thinks his or her kid can do no wrong, but give your child the benefit of the doubt and listen to his or her side of the story.

Or maybe your spouse has a dispute with a friend or neighbor. You may not agree with their side of the argument, but supporting and defending your spouse is far more important than "being right" about any isolated incident. In the long run, your loyalty will strengthen the relationship.

5

Discipline

Self-discipline is a form of
freedom. Freedom from laziness and
lethargy, freedom from expectations
and demands of others, freedom from
weakness and fear—and doubt.
—Harvey Dorfman,
Sports Psychologist

Good Things Don't Come Easy

If you want to achieve a goal, you have to want it badly enough. You have to endure. You have to put up with the setbacks, the disappointments, the heartbreaks and persevere. Perhaps Satchel Paige summed it up best: "Ain't no man can avoid being born average, but there ain't no man got to be common."

Satchel Paige wanted to be in the majors, but when he was a young man, African Americans were not allowed in the majors. So for 20 years he played in the Negro Leagues, traveling from one small town to another, sleeping on the bus because blacks were not allowed in hotels, eating baloney sandwiches because blacks were not allowed in restaurants. He put up with segregation and racism for 20 years, until he finally made the majors at age 42, and then went on to pitch effectively for five years!

Ryne Duren was a hard-throwing pitcher in the late 1950's and early 60's. As a teenager, a severe case of rheumatic fever left him legally blind. In fact, an eye specialist advised Duren to give up baseball.

"I was not going to let my vision stand in the way of my dream," said Duren. He began wearing thick-lensed glasses and tinted sunglasses, which later became a trademark of his in the major leagues.

Duren labored in the minor leagues for eight years. "The combination of my eyesight and the poorly lit minor league ballparks made it very difficult for me to see the catcher's signs."

But Duren persisted and eventually became one of the top relievers in baseball. But then another demon–alcoholism–haunted him, finally forcing him to retire.

Without baseball, Duren went into a full tailspin. His wife left him because of his excess drinking. He then squandered all his money, and was committed to the Texas State Mental Hospital less than six months after his last game with the Senators.

After more years of alcoholism and suicide attempts, Duren went to DePaul Hospital in Milwaukee where he underwent 22 months of treatment that enabled him to turn his life around.

From 1968 until his death in 2011, Duren served as an addiction counselor for numerous agencies, foundations, and hospitals where he worked with adolescents and adults and taught them about the dangers of alcohol.

So in the pursuit of your goals and dreams, the question becomes, how badly do you want it? How much are you willing to sacrifice? Very few people are born with enough brains or talent to be successful without a lot of hard work. If there is something you want, other people are going to want it too, many of whom will have the same abilities as you. What separates the winners from the losers? In the end, the ones who achieve their goals are the ones who want them the most and work the hardest to attain them.

Wait for Your Pitch

You have three strikes before you strike out. You don't have to swing at the first pitch, and often times it's best not to, especially in your first at bat of a game. Take your time; see what kind of stuff the pitcher has. Figure out what you like to hit and let go what's not in your "sweet spot" until there are two strikes and you have to protect the plate. Ignore temptation; don't succumb to the pressure. All-time hitting experts Ted Williams and Rogers Hornsby's number one rule was "get a good pitch to hit."

Plate discipline may be the most difficult skill to learn in baseball, but it also may be the most valuable, and it's your mind not your body that performs it. Practice self-discipline at the plate, and it will become much easier to do in life, too.

It Ain't Over Till It's Over

Yogi Berra's most famous quote is probably "It ain't over till it's over," and that is so true. In baseball and in life, never assume a win until the last out is made.

In baseball, maybe you score three runs in the first and two in the second and start high-fiving. Next, without being aware of it, you relax a little, you start to get cocky, your celebration lights a fire under the opponent. Things start to go wrong, and the other team catches up and wins. Or you hit a bases-clearing double, stand in the middle of the diamond pumping your fists, and the next inning drop a fly ball.

Then there is the fan whose team gets ahead and starts trash talking his friends who are rooting for the other team. Next, as if scripted, the fan's team blows the lead, and the guy gets laughed out of town.

When you celebrate too early, you anger the Baseball Gods. Some would say you are jinxing yourself or your team. The classic example is not saying "no-hitter" when a pitcher has a no-hitter going. Believers cringe when the announcer talks about it. Invariably, as soon as he does—boom—a base hit, and no more no-hitter.

Pirates announcer Jim Rooker certainly knows what I'm talking about. On June 8, 1989, the Pirates scored 10 in the first against the hapless Phillies. Rooker announced, "If we don't win, I'll walk back to Pittsburgh." Unfortunately for Rooker and the Pirates, after six innings it was 11-10 Phils, who then tacked on five more to end up winning big.

True to his word, in October, Rooker walked from Philadelphia to Pittsburgh to raise money for charity.

If you're a ballplayer, once you start celebrating early, even if only in your head, there is a good chance you will let your guard down and stop playing your best. You will lose some of your focus, inspire the opponent, maybe all of the above. The bottom line is, play hard through every at-bat, every inning, every game, right to the end.

This lesson is so important: In baseball and life, we need to stay humble, to stay within ourselves, to keep our eye on the prize and not let up until the prize is ours. There will be plenty time to celebrate then and it will feel so much better.

Don't Beat Yourself

Connie Mack said, "I guess more players lick themselves that are ever licked by an opposing team. The first thing any man has to know is how to handle himself."

Jim Abbott, a successful major league pitcher despite being born with only one full arm, concurred when he said, "I worked very hard. I felt I could play the game. The only thing that could stop me was myself."

Good teams do not beat themselves. They don't drop pop ups, they don't get thrown out on poor base running plays, they know how to bunt, make all the plays in the field. Oftentimes, the best teams commit the fewest errors, do the simplest things well, run the bases well, and make minimal mental mistakes. They know where to throw the ball; they hit the cutoff man. You get the idea.

But often in the outside world, this simple rule is not followed. Who among us has not had one of those meals at a restaurant where the waiter was nowhere to be found, the wrong order was brought, or the utensils were dirty?

A restaurant can spend thousands of dollars trying to generate business. They could blanket the city with ads, offer drink specials, discounts, whatever, but marketing investments won't help them if they do not do the small things well. Then, they are beating themselves.

As with a ballclub where a manager needs to teach his team the right way to play, places like restaurants need toscreen and train their employees thoroughly, be organized and clean, and must be watchful to not let their high standards slip. In any competitive situation—whether it be in school, at a restaurant, or in baseball—you have to do the small things well so you don't beat yourself.

Pride Goeth Before a Fall

Whitey Herzog told this story about New Athens, Illinois, where he grew up: "We've got more taverns than grocery stores. One night, when I was a kid, I walked in, threw down a bill, and said, 'Give everybody a drink.' Nice gesture I thought, but down the bar somebody yelled, 'Hey big shot, your brother is still a better ballplayer than you are.'"

J. B. Durbin is a pitcher drafted by the Minnesota Twins. One spring training game, after getting three outs in a row, Durbin walked into the dugout and bragged, "You have just seen the Real Deal." The Real Deal then spent the next eight years bouncing between the minors, independent, Japanese, and Mexican leagues, never making The Show, and never living down the "Real Deal" nickname he had earned.

Smart players don't brag about their accomplishments because they know the next game they might strike out three times or throw the ball over the first baseman's head.

Be careful about shooting off your mouth. No one likes a braggart, and chances are, tooting your horn will come back and bite you on the butt.

Prove Yourself Every Day

Hall of Famer Carl Hubbell said, "A fellow doesn't last long on what he has done. He has to keep on delivering." Baseball players know that yesterday's boxscore is now lining a birdcage somewhere. The pitcher who wins on Opening Day could lose his next five starts and be back in the minors by June.

Proving yourself every day applies to work and relationships as well. Many divorces occur because one partner doesn't appreciate his or her spouse, makes no effort to show his or her devotion and love on a daily basis.

When you coast along at a job or on a team, someone else might be taking a class or doing extra workouts that will allow him to pass you on the org chart. The world does not sit still, and you cannot either. "What have you done for me lately" is a phrase that applies to every aspect of life.

Timing Is Everything

A common saying in baseball is that good hitting requires good timing, and good pitching disrupts that timing. This also applies to many other areas of the game. If you are winning by eight runs in the seventh inning, don't argue with an umpire if he makes a bad call; don't steal second or take an extra base. Doing so will only make you look like a bad sport, and you will probably lose your next argument with that ump and motivate the other team.

The same is true in life. If your wife has been working all day and then gets home late due to a flat tire, is it really wise to ask, "What's for dinner, honey?"

You Set the Tone

I've written speeches for CEOs, and several have told me they expect their managers to always be on time. They believe that managers set the tone of the workplace by their actions, not their words. If you expect everyone to be at their desk at eight in the morning but you straggle in at 10, aren't you really telling them it is okay to be late? Either you'll have no one's respect, or considered a hypocrite. Either way, you undermine your own authority.

As a baseball coach or a top player, you need to set the tone the same way, *show* your teammates what is expected. Don't just tell them. If they are expected to be at every game and hustle at all times, you have to always be there and always give 100%. Lead by example and you are much more likely to be followed.

Take Care of Your Equipment and It Will Take Care of You

When I was growing up, my father would occasionally pick up my glove, toss it at me, and say, "Oil it." So I would go get the jar of Vaseline and rub it into the glove. My father's message was simple. He hated to see gloves with dry, cracked leather.

A dried-up glove is a sign of an uncommitted player, not to mention making fielding a lot more difficult. The ball doesn't stick in a stiff glove the way it does with a well-oiled and cared-for one.

The same is true with bats. Players who really care about their hitting keep their bats close to them and take good care of them.

What does a neglected glove or bat say about a ballplayer? Maybe he should be doing something else, because chances are he's not as good a player as he could be, nor will he ever be.

Are there things in your life that need your attention, that need to be maintained? Are there aspects of your life that have fallen into disrepair, that make it look like you don't care? Show the world and yourself what is important to you; give those things the time, attention, and respect they deserve, and they will become even more meaningful parts of your life.

Be Organized

If you are playing first base, when you come off the field, put a ball in your glove. That way, you won't waste time next inning looking for a ball for warmups. Keep track of the batting order so you can be prepared mentally and physically each time you go to the plate.

Clean up after yourself: Your mother is not in the dugout. After the game, throw away all the water bottles and gum wrappers, put away the helmets and the catcher's gear. Make sure you have all your equipment and no one else has left behind his or hers either.

When good organizational skills become second nature, you can devote your time and energy to important things, like your skills, your teammates, tomorrow's game.

Needless to say, being organized extends to real life and your job as well. A recent study from Express Employment Professionals showed that more than 50% of business leaders said that huge amounts of productivity are lost due to a lack of organization.

Disorganization costs companies money in lost hours and missed opportunities. According to the survey, disorganized employees who earn $50,000 a year can cost companies an estimated $11,000 a year in lost hours. Whether it's desk clutter, avalanches of emails piling up, or lack of proper planning, poor time management can hurt the entire company.

Identify Wasted Time

Practices tend to be short, especially in the lower leagues, and they should be, as it is tough to get any kid younger than 10 to focus on anything for more than an hour. Yet bad coaches waste time in practice. For instance, how many times have you watched infield practice and the catcher just stands there and hands the ball to the coach. How does this improve the catcher's skills? Have infielders take turns handing the ball to the coach. Then the catchers can work on blocking pitches in the dirt. Or if you have two players per infield position, have them hit grounders to each other. (This works best with older players!)

Stop and think. Where are you wasting time? Are there chunks of time during which you regularly are doing nothing? Are there distractions that regularly take you away from what you should be doing, like surfing the web or playing games on your computer or phone? Do you have work or study habits that you follow only because that's how you've always done things, not because it is efficient?

Know When the Moment Is Right

There is an appropriate time when people are ready, and have the greatest ability to, learn. For example, I have always been wary of teaching the curve ball to 13- and 14-year-old pitchers. It is terrible timing for a number of reasons.

First, young teenagers are in the midst of transitioning from the 46' Little League distance to the plate to the full 60'6". Adding a breaking ball only adds to the physical stress. Secondly, young pitchers' fingers are smaller and they have trouble gripping a curve. Because their hands are not fully developed, they are more likely to injure themselves. In addition, when a young pitcher has some success with a curve ball, he tends to throw it too often, at the expense of developing arm strength and command.

Or maybe there is a young hitter whom the coach wants to move to the middle of the lineup? Are they mentally prepared for the added responsibility?

Look around at your job or in your home. Is there someone your company is trying to bring along but who might not yet be ready for the added responsibility? The question needs to be asked, what is best and realistic for that person at that time, regardless of what the company wants to happen. Are they ready? If not, it could be a case of one step forward and three steps backward.

And later, when they are ready, maybe that initial bad experience will have turned them off from the new responsibility, or maybe their confidence will have been hurt and they don't do as well as they should.

The same applies to relationships. Both people have to be emotionally prepared to take the next step, and can't be forced into a deeper commitment. Forcing the situation is like forcing a young pitcher to throw a curveball, which will likely cause injuries later in the relationship.

6

Cooperation

Finding good players is easy. Getting
them to play as a team is another story.
—Casey Stengel

Trust Others

As a pitcher, you know your abilities, you recognize batters and know *their* abilities, you have ideas, and you want to win, sometimes by yourself.

Pitchers stand on the mound by themselves, and sometimes they think it's up to them to win the game themselves. But ultimately, baseball is a team sport. On the mound, you have to be willing to listen to your catcher. He may know something about the opposition or the situation that you don't. He probably knows something about you that you don't, or can see something about how you are pitching that you can't.

The minute you start to think you can win a game yourself is the minute you set off on a course towards losing. A catcher might call a pitch that turns into a home run, or a fielder might let a ball go through his legs, but everyone is doing the best he or she can, and you are not above making mistakes either.

You have to trust people enough to listen to them, trust them enough to let the batter hit the ball so your fielders can make the plays. You can't strike out everyone anyway. And if they make the wrong call or drop the ball, you also have to be willing to back them up no matter how disappointed you are, and trust them again next time. At the end of the day, you're all playing for the same team, striving for the same goals. You can't win without them, and they can't win without you.

Support Your Teammates

One spring after his Indians had underachieved the season before, Albert Belle said, "We need to start acting like a team, focus on winning and not worry about all of the other stuff that goes on. We lost our focus last year. We worried about who was being hired, who was being fired. That's got to change. We don't need any more finger pointing. We need to act like a team."

People make mistakes. In baseball and life. Do not rub their faces in the mistakes they make. If you must say something, say something positive, encourage them. It's one of your jobs as a player on a team. And just as your teammates need support when they do not succeed, so will you when you strike out or make a big error.

Teams Win and Lose Together

If a teammate drops a ball and the winning run scores, don't blame him. How did the other runners get on base leading up to the error and how many opportunities to score or prevent more runs were missed? You got the game-winning hit? That doesn't make you the hero; you're just part of the winning equation. Who did you drive in?

A lot of factors go into winning and losing a ballgame. Neither ever comes down to just one incident. So it is wrong to pile a lot of credit or blame onto one event in a game, good or bad. Success and failure are always a combination of many factors. Keep that in mind and you will be a better teammate, and your team will be more successful.

Being a team player can also be your fast track to success in business. When I work as a speechwriter for CEOs, they always share what they look for in an employee. Once I was interviewing a CEO and he walked over to a cabinet and pulled out a file thick with emails, reports, and memos. He said to me, "I have over 6,000 employees, and I can't track them all. But I do see a lot of reports come across my desk, and I look for one main thing. How many times does the writer say 'I,' and how many times does the writer say 'we,' and then give credit to the team he worked with? That team player is the one I tell my managers to keep promoting."

It Hurts to Let People Down

Maybe the mantra "do your best" should be changed to "do your best for your team."

When I was in fourth grade, I played center field for our Little League team. We needed one out to win. A fly ball was hit to me, an easy fly ball, and I dropped it. Our team lost. I was crushed. I went home and cried. My dad came up to my room and wondered why I was so upset. He explained to me that one person never loses a game. I made an error, but how about the kid who struck out when the bases were loaded, the kid who walked three batters in a row, or the kid who was thrown out trying to steal. We could blame them for losing the game. They made mistakes, too.

I looked at my father and said, "But I let my teammates down." And my father said, "If everyone felt that way, this world would be a better place."

Everyone Has to Row

When the Twins won the 1987 World Series, a lot of credit deservedly was given to manager Tom Kelly's dedication to teamwork. Kelly would say, "There's 25 of you guys rowing this boat, and if one of you guys drops your oar we're going to sink. Every single one of you is going to help float this river for 162 games. So don't be the guy who drops your oar."

Kelly's players really respected him and played hard for him, and a lot of players pushed past what was expected of them and did more. Kelly was the guy steering the boat, and his players just kept rowing—all the way to the World Series title.

Are you rowing in sync with everyone, or are you making the boat go in circle? Are you pulling hard whether you're the lead oarsman or the 25th player? A successful team or company or family requires everyone to work together and to do his or her best—from the top all the way to the bottom.

Learn the Culture

When you get hit by a pitch, don't rub the spot. Never talk about a no-hitter. Don't step on the foul lines when running off the field.

Are these things logical? No. Many cultural traditions are not logical, yet people follow them, and expect you to do the same. It is part of the fabric that weaves us together. Don't be a robot, but respect and learn the culture you are part of. You will earn the respect of those who preceded you because you will be showing respect for them and the world you are now a part of. You will also gain insights into the people and circumstances of your life.

Baseball has an entire language. There's no better entry into the culture of baseball than learning that language. As Ed Lynch, a former major league pitcher said, "The bases were drunk, and I painted the black with my best yakker. But blue squeezed me, and I went full. I came back with my heater, but the stick flares one the other way and chalk flies for two bases. Three earnies! Next thing I know, skipper hooks me and I'm sipping suds with the clubby."

Mr. Lynch went on to become a lawyer.

We All Need a Third Base Coach

Everyone needs help now and then. Only a fool does not seek it out. Base running provides a valuable example. You're on second, and there's a single to center. Your job is to score if you possibly can. You can't stop and look over your shoulder to see where the ball landed or how the outfielder is playing the ball. Your focus must remain forward. You have to pick up the third base coach to know what to do. He will tell you to hold at third or keep running to home.

If you turn around to the outfield so you can make the decision yourself, not only will it slow you down, you won't have the benefit of the coach's perspective, who can see the whole play.

When things are difficult or you have a problem, don't be afraid to ask for help and guidance, or be too cocky to think you don't need it. Your friends and family, a colleague or a teammate—like a good third base coach—may see the whole field better than you can, and help you get beyond your narrow perspective to a solution.

Show Respect

The word that will get you ejected from a ballgame is not what you might think it is. It's "you." Launching criticisms at people rather than their actions or words will result in resentment and reprisals. Life is the same way. When there is a problem, never blame the other person directly. Don't say to an umpire, "You made a terrible call." Criticize the call, don't attack the individual. Say, "I think that was the wrong call."

Attack the problem, not the person. Putting someone on the spot just puts the individual in the defensive, though their reaction might be an aggressive one.

How many times in life do you blame another person when something goes wrong? It's your wife's fault you got lost? You didn't get the promotion because your boss is unfair? Your girlfriend isn't holding up her end of the relationship? Don't point fingers and don't dump off blame. When there's a problem, it's far more productive and beneficial to discuss it and work towards a solution. Blaming someone else might make the problem that much worse, and will keep you from growing as a person on those oh-so-rare occasions when you might actually not be right.

Reach Out to See Within

Willie Mays said, "I'm a very lucky guy. I had so many people help me over the years that I never had many problems. If I had a problem, I could sit down with someone, and they would explain the problem to me, and the problem became like a baseball game."

Cliché time: "No man is an island." Frequently in baseball, despite Satchel Paige's cheerful reminder that "home plate don't move," a pitcher can't throw strikes or loses power on his pitches. As is often the case, the pitcher may be too close to the problem to see what he is doing wrong. He can try to correct it himself, but that is tough for any of us to do, to take a hard look at ourselves and see what needs to be changed. That is when you should seek help, an outside expert.

In the pitcher's case, it is the pitching coach. Pitching is much more complicated than many of us realize, even pitchers. A common problem they run into is flying open too soon. Pitchers must stay closed, that is, keep their front shoulder pointing at the target, until the stride foot plants. Doing so will result in a stable base and will cause his lead elbow, shoulders, and throwing arm to align with the plate. Only when your stride foot is planted should you "open up."

While flying open is a fundamental problem for pitchers, one most have some familiarity with, it is difficult for them to realize when they are doing it because it may seem to them they are just getting a little "something extra" on

their pitches by thrusting forward hard. They need someone outside their situation who can observe the problem
and point it out to them.

We all face situations like this—problems too close to
us for us to see—which is why counselors exist and why
having close friends and family who can be honest with
you is so important. Whether our problem is work- or
family-related, we are often too close to it or too deep into
the midst of it to see the problem, let alone "fix it." That
is when we all need our own pitching coach and must seek
outside help.

Remember, Everyone Is Biased

Two sayings on this concept are tied to baseball. "Where
you sit depends on where you stand," and "Never ask the
barber if you need a haircut." Everyone brings his or her
own perspectives to problems. I remember once when the
Orioles were playing the Yankees. My friend, a big O's
fan, watched his team lose two in a row to the Yankees.
Because he was an Oriole fan, his viewpoint was "The

Orioles always find a way to lose." As a Yankee fan, I saw it differently: "The Yankees always find a way to win," I explained.

It is important in our efforts to find happiness and better ourselves that we seek advice and input from others. But be sure to keep in mind to whom you are asking your questions. Remember, people see life through their own prisms, and often speak and act in their own self-interest, even if they are not aware of it. What is best for them may not be what is best for you.

7

Courage

Baseball is the exponent of American courage,
confidence, combativeness, American dash,
discipline, determination, American energy,
eagerness, enthusiasm, American pluck,
persistence, performance, American spirit,
sagacity, success, American vim, vigor, virility.
—Al Spalding

Confrontation Can Be Good

As a coach or a manager at a company, confrontation can be good. It shows your players or staff you will back them up, and it shows the other party you will stand up for yourself. Okay, you know that the umpire made the right call, yet your player is hopping mad and arguing that he was safe. You have no choice; you must back your player up to show him that you are on his side, that he can depend on you no matter what.

A good confrontation can spark a team or bring a department together. When my players were dragging and didn't have that spirit and drive we needed to succeed, I'd always inject some energy by arguing with an umpire.

Let's say you're on base and the shortstop tags you right on your nose. Don't get up and punch him, but don't forget either. Look for a chance to slide into him again, or if that doesn't come up, maybe it will with the third baseman or a fat fastball the next time you are up.

Show your opponents and your teammates you won't be pushed around, and you will earn their respect. The other guys will probably pick on someone else next time, and you will have shown yourself to be one of the leaders of your team.

A confrontation also serves the purpose of showing people that you have principles and beliefs that you are true to. Letting things slide conveys the opposite—that you are malleable, even weak. People who count on you will gradually lose confidence, and your opponents and competitors may be emboldened to push you even harder the next time.

Know Where the Wall Is

Bob Uecker said, "I knew when my career was over. In 1965, my baseball card came out with no picture on it." Sometimes it is just time to quit crashing into walls. You're not going to crash through one to make a catch.

If you are in the outfield chasing a long fly ball, put your arm out as you get close to the wall. Try to sneak a peak as you pursue the ball. Learn when you are going to crash into the wall, and don't be a fool trying to do the impossible. You'll only hurt yourself and possibly your team.

The same thing goes in life. Everyone has limits, and sometimes it is best to cut your losses or cash in your chips and wait for the next fly ball.

Sometimes the hardest thing to do is to admit you are wrong or made a mistake, or to admit your own limitations. Maybe that other guy deserved the promotion more than you did. Maybe you need help to repair the leaky sink or shovel the driveway. Know where your wall is and don't crash through it.

A classic example of not accepting one's limitations is the player who hangs on too long. As otherworldly as Babe Ruth was during his illustrious career, it is painful to think he was a shell of his former self in his final season, and that he did not retire a Yankee. In 1935, Ruth hit .181 with six home runs and 12 RBI for the Boston Braves. The Bambino would have been wise to retire the year before on a high note, when he swatted .288 with 22 home runs and 84 RBI for the Bronx Bombers.

Another example of a player that hung on too long, and there are many, is Derek Jeter. The Captain reached 3,000 hits in 2011, and his 2014 All-Star nod was more tribute than it was his for playing ability at that point. In the final two seasons of his career, Jeter hit a paltry .250 and had a combined offensive wins above replacement (WAR) of -0.5 and a defensive WAR of -1.0.

Fading ballplayers are often victims of the egos and drive that helped get them to the top. For the rest of us, often the culprit is laziness or fear of what lies beyond. We don't want to admit that maybe we need to learn new skills or look for a new job, or maybe we should end that relationship because the other person simply is not going to change. We stay in dead-end relationships and jobs because we refuse to accept we have hit a wall and it is time to move on.

Pick Your Battles

Don't fight every bad call. Just do so every now and then. But remember, the umpire is always right, even when he isn't. There is a lesson in the foolishness of fighting authority here. Learn it.

Two events in my life stand out that taught me to pick and choose my battles. My grandfather was married for over 50 years, and before I got married he wrote me a letter that contained one simple piece of advice. He said, "The secret of a successful marriage is knowing when to shut up and walk away." Well said, and enough said.

The other memorable lesson came when I was working for a large corporation as a speech writer. The company brought in some consultants to help them do some layoffs. Now if I had shut up, I probably would not have been laid off. But the consultants and their babbling corporate-speak drove me crazy.

So I wrote an article for the *Wall Street Journal* mocking the "consultant-speak" that rained all around me. One paragraph read as follows:

"It was insidious. You couldn't sit in the cafeteria without hearing about accelerated cultural change, cultural interventions, three-stream models, architectural rigor and discipline, people value, integrated strategic change, and core efficiencies. Managers would chat happily for hours, a glazed, contented look on their faces, while they chowed down their "cultural vitamins."

The upshot was that because of my lack of wisdom in picking and choosing my battles, I was laid off, with a non-working wife and two kids. Lesson learned.

Don't Be Intimidated

Don Drysdale said, "The pitcher has to find out if the hitter is timid, and if he is timid, he has to remind the hitter he's timid."

Richie Ashburn recalled, "I had a good look at the first pitch I ever saw from Drysdale. If I had not ducked, it would have hit me right between the eyes."

Frank Robinson used the mental challenge to his advantage. "Pitchers did me a favor when they knocked me down. It made me more determined. I wouldn't let that pitcher get me out. They say you can't hit if you're on your back, but I didn't hit on my back. I got up."

Who owns the plate, you or the pitcher? Once the pitcher intimidates you, you've lost. He is the bully and you are letting yourself be the victim. A player slides into second base with his spikes high, trying to disrupt your throw to first.

Handle the situation: Touch the bag and throw to first. Don't let yourself be overwhelmed or intimidated. If it happens, learn from your mistake and don't let it happen again. Stand up for yourself. If you don't, it will be to do so when you are challenged in the future.

Want To Be in the Action

If you are in the field praying they don't hit the ball to you, what will happen when they do? If you're on deck hoping the inning will end, how well will you do when the batter ahead of you reaches base? If you are afraid of the ball being hit to you or afraid of the pitcher's fastball, should you even be playing baseball?

Look at your own life. Are you hoping your boyfriend does not drop by? What does that tell you about the relationship? Are you praying your boss does not give you a challenging assignment? What does that tell you about your career? Are you dreading that the teacher may assign a paper? What does that say about your academic strength? If you do not want to be in the action, you're either in the wrong game or need to take a hard look at yourself, or both.

Take control of your life; don't let circumstances control you. Many of the most successful people in all walks of life—the top executive, the star player, the guy with the hottest girlfriend—are successful for no other reason than that they are not afraid. They squash down their fear and doubts with confidence and action. And the more they do it, the more being self-assured becomes the norm, and the easier it is to do.

So don't be intimidated. Stand close to the plate and get your swings in.

Take Chances

You can't steal second with a foot on first. Take a big lead every now and then. Nothing is guaranteed. You may get thrown out. But you might not, and next time you might take even a slightly bigger lead.

Working on a new pitch? Try it during the game. If you've been struggling on the mound, what do you have to lose? Maybe you'll take the batter by surprise, and you'll give him something else to think about. Maybe that new pitch will take you to the next level. You'll never know unless you try.

Another example of taking chances involves bunting, or trying something drastically different at the plate. With all the shifts in baseball these days, and nearly half the field vacated, what do you have to lose by trying to bunt it down the third base line? Even if you're not successful the first time, you'll give your opponents something to think about, and make it that much easier for yourself to try it again, or try something else outside your comfort zone.

Nothing Happens Until the Ball Moves

Let's start with some facts about the baseball—the magic sphere around which the magic game of baseball is played. In the history of the major leagues, over 75 different types of balls have been used. The last change to baseballs occurred in 1974 when the covering was changed from horsehide to cowhide.

Major League Baseball puts its baseballs through stringent testing before game use. They are shot from an air cannon at a speed of 85 feet per second at a wall of northern white ash and must rebound at no more than 57.8% of their original speed. Official Major League baseballs must weigh between 5 and 5¼ ounces and have a circumference between 9 and 9¼ inches. Between five and six dozen baseballs are used during each baseball game on average. One ball lasts an average of six pitches. The home team has to have 90 new baseballs on hand for each game.

But one fact stands above all others. As long as the ball is in the pitcher's hand, nothing will happen. Nothing happens until a pitch gets thrown and someone hits it.

What ball in your life are you holding onto, afraid to let go of it? What pitch are you afraid to make?

How many times do you sit quietly in class while someone else answers a question you know the answer to? How many Saturday nights are you home because you were afraid to ask the cute girl out on a date? How much happiness and success are you missing in your life because you are frozen on the sidelines, not taking part in the game?

Wind up and let the ball fly. The batter may hit it or the batter may strike out. Either way, you'll feel more alive and happy with yourself because you tried.

Be Aggressive

Are you the person no one calls back? Are you the one who tends to get ignored and bypassed? Maybe you are not being aggressive enough. There is a lot of truth to the old saying "the squeaky wheel gets the grease." Imagine you're a runner on first base. You don't take a lead. You don't make the pitcher throw over. The pitcher insults you by not even looking over. Why? As far as he can tell, you don't even care about advancing to second. He doesn't have to worry about you.

But what if you take a good-sized lead and dance farther out after each pitch? Now the pitcher has to pay attention to you. What if you fake a steal? Then the pitcher has to be really concerned. Plus, you are helping the hitter by disrupting the pitcher's concentration.

Are you just sitting on first base in your life? Is no one paying attention to you? Stuck in a relationship or job that is going nowhere? Whose fault is that? Try taking a lead, being aggressive, forcing the action. Show the world you want to advance and then go for it. Otherwise you will be seen as a lazy runner, clogging up the basepaths, not striving to score, content to spend your life on first base.

Be Decisive

This is rule number one for every umpire. Act like you are in charge. Don't take forever to call a player safe or out. Don't delay your ball/strike calls. If you do, people will question your judgment. One sign of indecisiveness from an umpire, and fans, managers, and players will be all over him.

The same is true in life. Parenting is the perfect example. What if you give your child an order, then rescind that order, then reinstate that order? What message are you sending your child? You're not sure you're right, so why should they listen to you?

Think about job interviews. Don't be timid and indecisive when speaking about yourself. Don't put yourself down or express self-doubt. If you don't have confidence in your abilities, prospective employers sure won't, either.

Know Thyself

The famous writer Chaim Potok once said, "A person must know who he is. A person must understand himself, improve himself, learn his weaknesses in order to overcome them. It is hard for a person to understand his own weaknesses."

Many kids blame the coach when they are on the bench or don't make the team, instead of taking an honest look at themselves. Maybe the problem isn't the coach, it's you. Did you hustle in practice? Are you only a one- or two-tool player? Do you need to develop bat speed, take more ground balls, strengthen your arm?

In short, be honest with yourself. How did your skills compare with the other players who were trying out? What are your weaknesses and what can you do to improve?

Remember, when something is not the way you would like it to be, look inward, not outward.

This rule, of course, applies in all other areas in life, too. Are you blaming the other person for a bad relationship? Did you really deserve an A on that project? Why not? What can *you* do to make yourself a better partner or student?

Know Your True Objective

Know your real objective and how to achieve it. For instance, a pitcher must understand his job is not to wear out his arm trying to strike out everyone. If you consistently try to overpower a batter, you may end up looking at a lot of three and two counts. You might be throwing six or seven pitches to every batter as you battle to strike them out.

Don't get caught up in that *mano a mano* stuff; don't let your vanity rule you. Your true objective is get the hitter out the quickest way possible. There is nothing wrong with throwing a sinker as the first pitch and getting the hitter to hit a grounder to second. That's a 1-pitch out that will help save your arm and keep your defense on its toes. Remember, your true objective is to get the batter to make an out, preferably early in the count. You have a team behind you with gloves on. Let them do their job.

Are you focusing on what you really want to achieve and not being sidetracked by an ego-driven quest, or distracted from your goal by trying to beat out someone for something? Stop and think. What is your true objective? What do you really want? Figure that out, make a plan for how to get it, and organize and direct your efforts to that end and to that end alone.

8

Growth

Without continual growth and progress,
such words as improvement,
achievement, and success have
no meaning.
—Benjamin Franklin

Set Attainable Goals

Mickey Rivers, if you could follow his logic, made some very interesting insights. For example, he once said, "I don't get upset over things I can't control, because if I can't control them there's no use getting upset. And I don't get upset over the things I can control, because if I can control them there's no reason to get upset."

What does this have to do with goals? Everything. I learned in college that I was not the hitter I thought I was. I was used to hitting .350, but playing at a higher level, I struggled to touch .250. Then my coach said something important to me: "Only bad hitters worry about their batting average."

The fact is you cannot make yourself get a hit. There are too many variables beyond your control. Someone can make a great catch; your line drive can go right at a fielder; a call can go against you; and sometimes the pitcher is just going to beat you. Your focus needs to be on things you can control, and your goals should be based on those things:

Get a good pitch to hit; take a good swing and time it right; run hard down the baseline.

Goals based on things you control are goals you can attain. And when you do, the end you are looking for, like a high batting average, has a good chance of happening. The same approach works in life. Reach for the stars, but don't focus on that castle in the sky. Identify the steps you need to take to get there, and climb them one at a time.

Think Small

If you find yourself behind, move deliberately to catch up. If your team is losing by six runs, don't try to get them back all at once. You can't hit a six-run homer. If it's the fourth inning, that is only a run an inning. That can be accomplished by bunting, stealing, hit-and-run, a sacrifice fly. Just do your job and let the next player do his, too. Build a ladder to success. Work to reach your goals a little at a time—one inning or one day at a time.

It's a lot like trying to get into shape. If you want to lose 30 pounds, it's not going to happen in a week, or even a month. Set an attainable goal, like two pounds a week. Mix in an exercise program and start slow—a one-mile walk, then two, maybe mix in a trip to the gym.

By setting realistic goals, you set yourself up to succeed, and once you start to succeed, it will make you feel good and you'll want to keep it going. If you try to do something all at once you will meet with frustration and be much more likely to give up.

Don't Dwell on Your Mistakes

Mistakes offer a learning experience. Don't beat yourself up. Learn the lesson and move on. As Sparky Anderson said, "People who live in the past generally are afraid to compete in the present. I've got my faults, but living in the past is not one of them. There's no future in it."

Tommy Lasorda hit the nail on the head when he said, "About the only problem with success is that it does not teach you how to deal with failure."

Don't run from your mistakes; grow from them. Take the lesson they offer, give yourself credit for trying, chalk

117

it up as an experience builder, and move on. Realize that you become a better person by learning from your mistakes and learning how to stop them from reoccurring. And of course, remember the words of Albert Einstein, who said, "Anyone who has never made a mistake has never tried anything new."

Adjust

Don't get locked into one way of doing things. Adjust to the pitcher's off-speed pitches or herky-jerky motion; adjust to the umpire's strike zone; shift your fielding position according to who is batting. Life and baseball are a series of small and large adjustments. If the umpire calls you out on a low strike, don't complain; make use of that knowledge next time you're up. If you get called out again on the same pitch, it is because you failed to adjust.

You may have figured out one way to do something and now always do it the same way. But are you sure it's the best way? Maybe moving out of your comfort zone will lead to improvements. What if the circumstances change?

Change is a constant in life. You need to change with the times, with all the circumstances that vary, or eventually you will get stuck in the rut you've created and the world will leave you behind.

Don't Allow Routine to Replace Thinking

Managers have a designated closer; they always bring in the same pitcher to get the last three outs. The problem with this? The closer may not always be the team's best option. Maybe the closer is tired or doesn't match up well against the opponent. Maybe splitting the role between two pitchers will make them both better. The best move yesterday may not be the best move today.

Too often managers establish a routine with their players and they simply stick with it, regardless of how guys are going and whether their strategy has been working lately. That way, the manager does not have to really think about options, make difficult decisions, run the risk of being

EVERYTHING I KNOW I LEARNED FROM BASEBALL

wrong and then criticized. He just points to the bullpen, and the closer trots out.

Always reconsider your decisions. Do not put your thought process on autopilot. What works in one situation may not work in another. It may take one thing to get you ahead, and something very different to keep you there.

Good Habits May Feel Bad While You Develop Them

The right way to do things often isn't what comes naturally. Players must be taught to round the bases touching the inside corner with their left foot. Why? Because hitting the inside of the bag with your left foot is awkward. But when you think about it, it makes sense. Doing so helps you make a tighter turn and keep your momentum going toward the next base, not the outfield. Staying inside the ball when hitting is another example. The temptation is to fly open, and when you connect the ball really goes, but without your front shoulder you can't reach the outside pitch or adjust to changeups.

Good habits have to be taught and repeated. Do them enough and enjoy the results and they won't feel awkward anymore. But be careful. Bad habits, like eating too much or watching too much TV, come to us easily. And once they are ingrained, it becomes that much harder for good ones to take their place.

Relearn

My father, a baseball coach for over 20 years, taught his granddaughter Jillian that it's OK to re-learn how it's done, whatever "it" may be. As Jillian said, "When I was in high school, he came to a practice to observe and ended up with me in the batter's box, teaching me an entirely new way to hold my elbow when I hit. It stopped practice, and I was, of course, embarrassed and annoyed. As every 14-year old girl would react, I thought I already knew how it was done. He re-taught me how to hit after I had batted one way for ten years. To no one's surprise but my own, it greatly improved my hitting."

Sometimes, even when you think you've got it all figured out and you're doing things the best way you can, you have to be willing to let someone stand in the batter's box with you, be a mirror for you to see yourself as you are, not as you think you are. As Earl Weaver famously said, "It's what you learn after you know it all that counts."

Keep Learning

Why are mentors necessary? They teach. Preston Wilson, former All Star, perhaps said it best when he said, "Baseball is this whole world of information; it's not just talent, it's information. The work is not always on the field, sometimes it's who you talk to and the information you gather. I remember being in the minor leagues and every time I saw someone that I respected or I liked from watching when I was younger or that I knew anything about the way they went about the game or their philosophies, I would ask them questions." Are you taking advantage of mentors, seeking out experts and asking questions? If not, are you really learning?

Adjust to New Technologies

When I began coaching summer league baseball, I noticed that a lot of kids were taking mighty swings at the ball and completely missing it. That is because of their coaches. Despite aluminum bats having been around for years, the coaches were still teaching kids the same hitting techniques they had since the 1950s.

Coaches preached to the kids that you had to really swing hard to get a good hit. You had to stride, open up your hips, and whip that bat through. The coaches had never adjusted to aluminum bats. The great thing about aluminum bats (for batters, anyway) is they are much livelier than wooden ones. You do not have to take a mighty swing to make the ball go far. You just have to make good contact, and chances are, even when you are jammed, the ball will pop over the second baseman's head for a Texas Leaguer.

So I let the kids take their mighty swings on the first two strikes, but on the third strike, they were not allowed to stride. They had to open up their stance, take no stride,

123

and just simply shift their weight while focusing on making contact with the ball. At first the kids were doubtful, as were the parents. But as the kids learned the contact approach to hitting, our team's overall performance at the plate drastically improved.

The point here? Aluminum bats had been around for years. But few coaches ever adjusted to the new "technology" when it took over the game. They made the mistake of not rethinking the way they had always done things.

What are you still doing the same old way, even though new technology may have made your approach obsolete, even though with a little training and practice you'll be doing things more quickly, more efficiently, better?

Have a Back-up Plan

In baseball, even when you make the right play, things don't always work out. That is why fielders serve as backups on every play. Pitchers back up plays at the plate; catchers and second basemen back up throws to first; outfielders charge the infield to back up the bases on stolen base attempts.

That is because sometimes things go wrong, even in the big leagues. Snagging an errant throw holds runners on their base and can even turn an error into an out.

Do you have a back-up plan for when things start to go wrong, when whatever you are doing is not working? Can you change your course of action to minimize the damage, to deal with an unforeseen event? Do you have someone who can step in and help you out when things do not go as planned?

9

Independence

Progress always involves risks. You can't
steal second base and keep your foot
on first."
—Frederick Wilcox

Find Your Strength

Jim Abbott, the former outstanding major league pitcher whose birth defect resulted in his having only a partial right arm, said, "There are millions of people out there ignoring disabilities and accomplishing incredible feats. I learned you can learn to do things differently, but do them just as well. I've learned that it's not the disability that defines you, it's how you deal with the challenges the disability presents you with. And I've learned that we have an obligation to the abilities we *do* have, not the disability."

People do have weaknesses and strengths. Figure out what yours are. Emphasize the latter and minimize the former. Don't be discouraged by the things you are not so good at, and don't let them get in the way of what you are good at. If you're not a power hitter, "hit them where they ain't." If you don't have a blazing fastball, work on your control and changing speeds. If your range in the field is limited, study the batters and work on getting good jumps.

Look for a Unique Edge

Pulling your pants legs down to your ankles may look cool, but what does it accomplish? Are you trying to follow the latest fashion or are you trying to win games?

Wear your socks high. It will make it harder for the umpire to call a low strike. And you might be more formidable in the eyes of your opponent if you stand out from the crowd.

Another unique edge is speed. Speed enables you to steal bases, beat out bunts, escape double plays, and a speed demon on base draws more pickoff attempts and is a distraction for the pitcher. Speed enables you to stretch a double into a triple, and in the outfield, speed enables you to chase down that fly ball.

Think of the real world. What companies use speed as a competitive advantage? Amazon Prime will deliver your package in two days, or less; UberEATS will pick up food from your favorite restaurant and deliver it in under 10 minutes; Jimmy John's is "freaky fast" and will deliver your food in 15 minutes or less.

Never stop thinking about what you need to do in school or at your job to gain and maintain an advantage. Don't just think about doing what is expected, though that is important, too. What are your own particular strengths and expertise that you could draw from to separate yourself from the pack?

Look at Things Differently

One of the most valuable forms of creativity is taking a fresh look at an old problem. The obvious, accepted solution is not always the best way. When I was a child, my father made weighted bats for on deck batters to use by pouring melted lead into them. Like everyone else in those days, he would drill a hole in the bat, melt the lead, and pour the lead into the bat and let it cool. A pretty involved process, but that's the way it was done.

Then Elston Howard, New York Yankees catcher and the first black player to play for that franchise, had a better idea, born, no doubt, during all that idle time catchers spend down in the bullpen. Elston thought, "Why bother drilling a hole in the bat and filling it with lead? Why don't we just make a lead donut and simply drop it over the bat?"

Bingo—it worked! Not only was the process made much easier, but players could now loosen up using their own bats. Drop the donut on while warming up, then take it off when it's time to hit. The point is, instead of just accepting the status quo, Elston Howard just looked at things in a different way and came up with a better way of doing something.

Do the same at your job or in your home. Pretend you are a visitor from a faraway place observing your habits and customs for the first time. Does it make sense to check emails every 10 minutes, or should you not interrupt your work so often? Should you cut the lawn diagonally instead of in short rows across it? You never know how or when a new idea will hit. Keep your mind open so you'll be paying attention when it does.

Try Something Different

If it ain't working, try something different. Don't get too attached to what you know, as comfortable as that may be, and don't give up. Tim Wakefield used that philosophy to propel a long, successful career as a pitcher. Wakefield was drafted as a first baseman in 1988 by the Pirates. Then a scout told him that with his skills he would never get out of the minor leagues. So Wakefield began developing the knuckleball. People thought he was crazy, but he just said, "I just want to be able to say I tried everything I could to make it."

The following season, Wakefield made his professional pitching debut for the Single A Salem Buccaneers. Wakefield kept working and kept improving, reaching the big leagues as a pitcher for the Pirates in 1992. In his major league debut, Wakefield threw a complete game against the St. Louis Cardinals, striking out 10 batters. He went on to post an amazing record of 8-1 that year in 13 starts, and then won two more games in the NLCS.

Don't put yourself in a box. Don't sell yourself short on what you can do. Success is about doing your best, but it's also about pushing your limits and trying new things.

Don't Compare Yourself to Others

Why aren't you blessed with an arm that can throw the ball 95 miles an hour? Why aren't you 6'4" with home run power? Why can't you go from home to first in 3.2 seconds? There are limits to everyone's abilities, and there is always someone who is better than you. Why get depressed or drive yourself crazy thinking about the skills you don't have?

I stand 5'7" on a good day and hardly looked like a ballplayer, even in my prime. In college I was a runt, 140 pounds tops. When I made my college team I was given number 4 because it was the smallest uniform they had, and I was the only one who could fit into it. I made the team because I focused on what I could do, not what I could not. I was nowhere near the skill level of my teammates, but no one wanted it more than I. I was small, so I learned how to work out walks. I was quick, so I learned how to bat left handed to give me the edge against righty pitchers and get me two steps closer to first base. I learned how to bunt and put the ball in play. And I practiced my fielding. A lot.

The point is, I didn't sit around and whine that I was not the biggest or fastest or strongest. I didn't feel sorry for myself. I took whatever steps I could to help me reach my goal of playing college baseball.

Ignore Conventional Wisdom

Sometimes conventional wisdom can get you killed. I was a catcher in college, 5'7" and around 140 pounds. Traditionally, in baseball it has always been the job of the catcher to block the plate.

Hello? I am a small man, and that guy barreling down the third base line headed for home is 6'2" and 190 pounds. If I block the plate, he fully intends to run me over. An injury is likely and getting the out doubtful.

Thinking about my physical disadvantage, it occurred to me that no other player besides the catcher blocks their base. No one else stands in front of the runner waiting to be knocked back to their ancestors. They stand on the side, and as the runner slides in, they tag him.

I explained this to my coach, who responded with a skeptical look. But I started to let the runner slide into home while I stood on the side and tagged him as he went by. This approach worked, and most importantly, at least to me, I was kept out of the emergency room.

Look around in your own life both on and off the field and think about what conventional wisdom you follow that perhaps really doesn't make sense for you or that doesn't fit your particular lifestyle. You should determine the best way to handle things and best paths to take based on your circumstances and personal situation, not on what everyone else does or says you should do.

You Can't Fake It

"You can't fake being there" is a quote by retired Marine Corps General, Charles C. Krulak. General Krulak said it, and my father embodied it. He was at every single pitching lesson my sister ever had, catching or chasing after her wild pitches and miserable change-ups, squatting on his knees without catcher's gear, putting up with her frustration and impatience for hours at a time. And the best part, always cheering her on.

His daughter said, "Never once did my father say a single negative thing to me during a pitching lesson. Never once did he let me leave discouraged. At the time, I always appreciated his positivity. Looking back on it now, I just appreciate his presence, that he was there. He taught me that as a father, even when you've had a bad day, or you think pitching lessons are expensive, or your daughter is driving you crazy by being a typical 15-year-old, you absolutely cannot fake being there."

Learn to Say "No"

An unwritten rule among many baseball players is, never let anyone borrow your glove. Your glove is broken in for your hand, formed the way you like it and the way that works best for you. When someone else uses your glove, they may stretch it out, crease it a different way, drop it in the dirt, whatever.

If the glove is returned to you "out of shape," it can be harder to restore it to the way you like it than it would be to break in a new glove. When it comes to lending out your glove, even though it might make you look selfish or unkind, and make you worry the person will be angry with you, the best answer to give is "No."

The same is true for anything that is precious to you—be it your equipment, a book you love, or even your time— you need to learn to say no for both your sake and the other person's.

Mix It Up

As I mentioned before, the only thing wrong with staying on the same track is that eventually you will get run over. Any good baseball player knows this. If you keep pitching fastball after fastball, especially in the same location, hitters will eventually just sit on your fastball, time it, and pound it over the fence. If you always go to the plate after throwing to first, runners will start taking off the next pitch after a pickoff attempt.

If, as a batter, you always look for the ball down and orient your swing that way, before long pitchers will catch on, and you'll be getting a steady diet of high hard ones. If you always pull, the fielders will bunch up and there will be nowhere for your hits to go through.

The same is true in how you approach your school work and relationships. As a student, it is critical to establish best practices and to follow them. But if you close your mind to adjusting and enhancing your approach, your performance will plateau, and you will fail to keep up with challenges and situations that are ever-changing.

Similarly, friends and family want consistency from you, but life and people themselves are so complicated, it is essential that you change and grow with time. Besides, variety is the spice of life. Too much of the same thing gets boring after a while.

Strive to Be a Big Leaguer

Always set high expectations for yourself. Perhaps this was best summed up by baseball manager Sparky Anderson who said, "I don't know whether I'm a big leaguer or not, but I want to find out, and if I can't do it, then I'll be a minor leaguer the rest of my life."

You can't reach your goals if you do not set them, and you'll never know how high you can reach if you don't try. Strive for the best and focus on the steps that will get you there. What do you need to do to be a big leaguer? And this is not just a baseball question: Whatever your profession, your hobby, whatever you enjoy doing—what do you have to do to reach the top, or at least to be the best you can be?

Being the best you can be is the definition of success, and you'll never get there if you don't aim high.

Develop Your Off-Speed Pitch

When a hitter is off balance, there are a lot of swings and misses. Even if he hits the ball, there is nothing behind the contact. A weak grounder or pop up results.

If you constantly pitch to the outside corner, batters will start to lean out there and become very comfortable at the plate. If you fall into a pattern, the element of surprise will be gone, and the batter will have a huge mental edge.

How are you mixing things up? Or are you just throwing the same pitch day after day, bringing nothing new to the table? How can your relationships, your career, your appreciation of life thrive without variety?

What is your strategy, your off-speed pitch that will surprise the competition, leave them swinging at air? What new thoughts and ideas are you bringing to your life and your relationships? The problem with staying on the same track, the saying goes, is sooner or later you're going to get run over.

Quotation
Sources

Page 1, **Ted Williams**, http://www.azquotes.com/quote/1306957

Page 3, **John Kieran**, http://www.sportsfeelgoodstories.com/lou-gehrig-the-iron-horse/

Page 3, **Casey Stengel**, http://www.baseball-almanac.com/quotes/hank_bauer_quotes.shtml

Page 5, **Dave Winfield**, http://www.brainyquote.com/quotes/quotes/d/davewinfie371510.html

Page 6, **Bob Feller**, https://books.google.com/books?isbn=0786488727

Page 8, **Bill Rigney**, https://www.baseballprospectus.com/article.php?articleid=9896

Page 17, **Earl Weaver**, https://books.google.com/books?isbn=1607090279

Page 19, **Dick Williams**, https://www.quotetab.com/quote/by-dick-williams.

Page 20, **Henry Aaron**, http://www.notable-quotes.com/a/aaron_hank.html

Page 22, **Mike Schmidt**, http://www.quotinq.com/quotes/499360

Page 31, **Roy Bennett**, https://twitter.com/ddctalent/status/729302168235352064

Page 34, **Yogi Berra**, http://parade.com/425204/alison-abbey

Page 35, **Satchel Paige**, http://www.satchelpaige.com/quote2.html

Page 47, **Joe Garagiola**, http://www.notable-quotes.com/b/baseball_quotes.html

Page 52-53, **Gary Carter**, https://quotefancy.com/quote/1735326/Gary-Carter

Page 63, **Harvey Dorfman**, https://www.goodreads.com/author/quotes/94734.H_A_Dorfman

Page 65, **Satchel Paige**, http://quotes.yourdictionary.com/author/satchel-paige/91821

Page 68, **Connie Mack**, http://www.jarofquotes.com/view.php?id

Page 69, **Jim Abbott**, http://www.worldofquotes.com/quote/56816/index.html

Page 72, **Whitey Herzog**, http://www.nyyfansforum.com/archive/index.php/t-25811.html

Page 71, **J.B. Durbin**, https://thecoggintoboggan.com/2015/01/30/obscure-philadelphia-athlete-of-the-week-jd-the-real-deal-durbin/

Page 72, **Carl Hubbell**, http://www.forbes.com/quotes/1401/

Page 81, **Casey Stengel**, http://www.caseystengel.org/

Page 84, **Albert Belle**, http://quotemaster.org/
Pointing+Fingers

Page 87, **Tom Kelly**, Tom Kelly Quotations.

Page 89, **Ed Lynch**, http://www.peterga.com/baseball/
quotes/malaprop.htm

Page 91, **Willie Mays**, http://www.achievement.org/
autodoc/halls/bus

Page 95, **Al Spalding**, http://www.quotehd.com/
quotes/words/persistency

Page 98, **Bob Uecker**, http://www.superiortelegram.
com/content/lance-and-billys-take-local-sports

Page 102, **Don Drysdale**, Source: *New York Times* (July 9,
1979)

Page 102, **Richie Ashburn**, https://www.newspapers.
com/newspage/120081416/

Page 102, **Frank Robinson**, http://www.biography.
com/people/frank-robinson-9460731

Page 109, **Chaim Potok**, http://www.goodreads.com/
quotes/7167949-a-person-must-know-who-he-is-a-person-
must

Page 113, **Benjamin Franklin**, http://www.brainy-
quote.com/quotes/keywords/growth.html

Page 115, **Mickey Rivers**, https://www.brainyquote.com/quotes/quotes/m/mickeyrive789951.html

Page 117, **Sparky Anderson**, http://thinkexist.com/quotation/people_who_live_in_the_past_generally_are_afraid/220569.html

Page 117, **Tommy Lasorda**, http://www.notable-quotes.com/l/lasorda_tommy.html

Page 118, **Albert Einstein**, http://www.woodwardenglish.com/never-made-mistake-einstein-quote/

Page 122, **Earl Weaver**, http://www.industryweek.com/blog/it-s-what-you-learn-after-you-know-it-all-counts

Page 122, **Preston Wilson**, http://www.perfectgame.org/articles/view.aspx?article=10486

Page 127, **Frederick Wilcox**, http://www.wisdom-quotes.com/quote/frederick-wilcox.html

Page 129, **Jim Abbott**, http://www.livingonehanded.com/sunday-quote-jim-abbott/

Page 133, **Tim Wakefield**, http://www.990wbob.com/sports/curtain-call-timmmay

Page 140, **Sparky Anderson**, http://www.memorable-quotations.com/anderson3.htm

Printed in the USA
CPSIA information can be obtained
at www.ICGtesting.com
LVHW091939170124
769250LV00010B/290

9 781938 545344